# THE STORY OF SPACE

# PROBES TO THE PLANETS

## STEVE PARKER

FRANKLIN WATTS
LONDON•SYDNEY

First published in the UK in 2015 by Franklin Watts

Franklin Watts
338 Euston Road
London NW1 3BH

Franklin Watts Australia
Level 17/207 Kent Street
Sydney, NSW 2000

Dewey classification: 629.4'35

A CIP catalogue record for this book is available from the British Library.

ISBN: 978 1 4451 4047 6

Franklin Watts is a division of Hachette Children's Books, an Hachette UK company.
www.hachette.co.uk

THE STORY OF SPACE: PROBES TO THE PLANETS
was produced for Franklin Watts by
David West 𝔁𝔁 Children's Books, 6 Princeton Court, 55 Felsham Road, London SW15 1AZ

Copyright © 2014 David West Children's Books

**IMAGE CREDITS**:
**ALL IMAGES COURTESY OF NASA EXCEPT:** p6tr, NASA/Max Planck, p6b, NASA Goddard Photo and Video; p7tr, NASA/Johns Hopkins University Applied Physics Laboratory, p7bl, NorJerry MagnuM Porsbjer; p8b, ESA - AOES Medialab; p10bl, ESA/MPS/DLR/IDA; p11m, p17br, p23bl, p27m, NASA/JPL; p12bl, NASA/USGS; p13tr, Jim Bell (Cornell University), Mike Wolff (Space Science Institute), and NASA; p15t, NASA/JPL (Corby Waste), p15mr, NASA-JPL-Cornell, p15ml, NASA/JPL; modified/coloured by D Mitriy, p15b, NASA/JPL-Caltech/USGS/Cornell University; p16l, NASA-JPL-Caltech-Malin Space Science Systems; p17ml. NASA - JPL-Caltech - Olivier de Goursac, p17m, b, NASA/JPL-Caltech/MSSS; p21tr, p24bl, NASA/JPL/Space Science Institute, p21r, SA/JPL/Space Science Institute; p22t, The Hubble Heritage Team (AURA/STScI/NASA); p24mr, NASA/JPL-Caltech/Space Science Institute; p25tr, NASA/JPL/University of Arizona, p25b, NASA/JPL-Caltech; p26t, NASA/Johns Hopkins Applied Physics Laboratory, p26l, NASA/JPL-Caltech/UCLA/MPS/DLR/IDA/PSI, p26br, Rick Sternbach/KISS, p26r, NASA/JPL/JHUAPL, p26bl, NASA, ESA, and A. Feild (STScI); p27 tl, Halley Multicolor Camera Team, Giotto Project, ESA, p27tr, br, ESA; p28tl, H. Weaver (JHU/APL), A. Stern (SwRI), and the HST Pluto Companion Search Team, p28t, Lunar and Planetary Institute, p28l, NASA/Johns Hopkins University Applied Physics Laboratory/Southwest Research Institute, p28r, C m handler; p29r, b, ESO-L. Calçada

Printed in China

# CONTENTS

*Space probe* Cassini *has been in orbit around Saturn since 2004, making hundreds of flybys of the giant planet and its dozens of moons.*

# INTRODUCTION

The Solar System is vast – 7.4 trillion kilometres (4.6 trillion miles) from the Sun to the outer reaches. Its eight planets, with their moons, are tiny specks spread far apart in the great emptiness. Our exploration of space, which began over 50 years ago, has mainly focused on these planets and moons.

We have overcome such gigantic distances by using unmanned probes. They fly close to planets and even land on them, gather data, record images and transmit the information back to Earth. Knowledge of other planets helps us to understand how our own planet came to be, how it is changing now and what might be waiting in the future.

*Mobile probes, like NASA's Mars explorer Curiosity, are called rovers. Partly remote controlled and partly robotic, they can explore a distant and hostile environment without the risk and expense of human spaceflight.*

# SOLAR PROBES

Categorised a 'yellow dwarf', our Sun is a medium-sized star halfway through its 10-billion-year life cycle. This huge body makes up almost 99% of the total mass of the Solar System that spins around it.

## INSIDE THE SUN

1. **CORE** Thermonuclear reactor
2. **RADIATIVE ZONE** Heat spreads outwards
3. **CONVECTION ZONE** Columns of heat rise and fall
4. **PHOTOSPHERE** Visible surface of the atmosphere
5. **CHROMOSPHERE** Thin layer of wispy hydrogen
6. **CORONA** Wide area of hot plasma radiating outwards

*In the 1970s–80s two Helios probes circled the Sun slightly within the orbit of planet Mercury, at record speeds of 252,000 km/h (157,000 mph).*

## EMPIRE OF THE SUN

Like all stars, the Sun began as a vast, intensely cold cloud of dust and hydrogen atoms. This collapsed inwards under its own gravity, clumped together, and ignited. The Sun is made of 74% hydrogen, 24% helium and 2% heavy elements. Its core pressure and temperature of 13 million °C (23 million °F) are high enough to rip apart hydrogen atoms and reform them as helium – a process called nuclear fusion. The incredible energy radiates outwards in columns to blaze on the photosphere as light and heat.

*NASA's SDO (Solar Dynamics Observatory) began probing the Sun's magnetic field and its various rays in 2010.*

*The Sun's charged particles meet Earth's magnetic field and cause polar lights or auroras (above). Plasma eruptions from its surface (right) can cause magnetic storms on Earth.*

The **SUN** is mainly **PLASMA** – neither a **gas, liquid** or **solid,** but more like **PURE ENERGY.**

# PROBING THE INFERNO

Probes have analysed the interior of the Sun and on its surface observed sunspots – magnetic storms larger than Earth. The surface of the Sun is 5,500 °C (10,300 °F) 'cool' enough to be approached by robot spacecraft. In 2018 Solar Probe Plus will become the most intrepid solar explorer yet. To study the outer corona up close, its instruments are protected by the shadow of a special carbon heat shield.

*Since 1995 NASA's Solar and Heliospheric Observatory, SOHO, has been sending real-time data on space weather – variations in the solar wind from the Sun.*

## SOLAR PROBE PLUS

1. **THERMAL SHIELD** Carbon composites
2. **PRIMARY SOLAR ARRAYS** For use early in the mission and then stowed behind the heat shield
3. **COMMUNICATIONS ANTENNA**
4. **SECONDARY SOLAR ARRAY** Liquid cooled, deployed on final approach to the Sun's surface

*Solar Probe Plus will speed around the Sun three times faster than the Helios craft.*

*The Sun throws out a huge arc of energy, or prominence, big enough to engulf all the planets. Surprisingly the Sun's visible surface, the photosphere, is hundreds of times cooler than the invisible corona that surrounds it.*

The **SUN**'s energy **particles** spend an **average** of **200,000 YEARS** travelling around **inside** their **star**, then after **RELEASE** they reach **Earth** in just **EIGHT MINUTES.**

# MERCURY

## INSIDE MERCURY

1. **CRUST** Up to 320 km (200 miles) thick
2. **MANTLE** Chiefly silicate rocky minerals
3. **CORE** Mainly liquid iron

**B**attered, scorched Mercury is the smallest planet in the Solar System. Closest to the Sun, its atmosphere boiled off long ago. This super-hot world is one of the most difficult and hazardous places a probe might visit.

*The first Mercury probe was Mariner 10 (left) in 1974. It photographed half the planet and discovered its magnetic field.*

TV cameras

Sun shade

**MERCURY** is **named** after the **ancient** Roman **MESSENGER** to the **GODS.** Its **year** (one Sun orbit) is **88** Earth **days**.

## BLASTED WORLD

The Sun shines on Mercury ten times more strongly than on Earth. The difference between night and day temperatures is the greatest in the Solar System, from -173 °C (-343° F), which would liquefy oxygen, to 421 °C (790 °F), which would melt lead. Mercury also rotates slowly, so one Mercurian day lasts 58 Earth days. Its large metal core makes it the second densest planet after Earth. However Mercury's small size means, unlike other planets, it could not hang onto any of its ancient atmosphere.

*So close to the Sun, Mercury is hard to observe from Earth. It is mostly seen in transit, or passing in front of, our blazing star.*

MMO Orbiter

Sun shield

Mercury Transfer Module

MPO Orbiter

*The joint ESA (European Space Agency) and JAXA (Japan Space Agency) probe BepiColombo should arrive on Mercury in 2022. On it, JAXA's Mercury Magnetospheric Orbiter (MMO) will analyse the planet's magnetic field while ESA's Mercury Planet Orbiter (MPO) maps the planet in greater detail than ever before.*

Ion engines

*Launched in 2004, NASA's MESSENGER probe made three flybys of the planet before becoming the first craft to orbit Mercury in 2011. Pulled in fast by the Sun, MESSENGER had to circle our star 15 times before it slowed enough to be caught by Mercury's weak gravitational field.*

*Having imaged all of Mercury's surface, MESSENGER's mission was extended from 2012 to search for water ice, thought to be hidden deep in polar craters.*

**MERCURY** is the most **CRATERED** **object** in the **SOLAR SYSTEM**.

## A MILLION HITS

Without an atmosphere to protect it, Mercury has born the full impact of every space object attracted onto its surface by the nearby Sun. Some were so big, they buckled the planet on the far side of their strike site. As well as documenting these scars, *MESSENGER* also discovered many volcanoes. Mercury holds vital clues to the origin of our Solar System's inner, rocky worlds.

*MESSENGER photographed Mercury's Caloris Basin in great detail. Caloris (here in yellow) is one of the largest impact craters in the entire Solar System. The orange splotches, lower left, show volcanic vents.*

# VENUS

**S**ometimes called 'Earth's evil twin', Venus hides its surface beneath thick clouds of sulphur fumes. It is the hottest planet in the Solar System – too scorching for any form of life.

## INSIDE VENUS

1. **ATMOSPHERE** 96% carbon dioxide, 3.5% nitrogen, particles of sulphur dioxide, droplets of sulphuric acid
2. **ROCKY CRUST** 90% resurfaced by molten lava
3. **MANTLE** Similar depth to Earth, 2,700 km (1,700 miles)
4. **CORE** Probably part-liquid and part-solid, possibly metallic

*ESA's Venus Express orbiter (below) reached the planet in 2006. Its long-term mission was to study Venus' atmosphere. The craft imaged cloud formations (inset), confirmed the presence of lightning and found evidence of recent volcanic activity.*

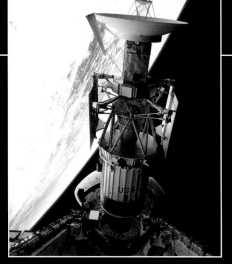

*NASA's Venus probe Magellan was launched by a Space Shuttle in 1989. By 1994 it had mapped 98% of Venus' surface using radar (radio waves) to see through the clouds.*

## UNDER PRESSURE

Venus is a similar size to Earth and has a similar mass and gravity, but crucially it lies closer to the Sun and has almost no magnetic field. For the first billion or so years of its life, Venus probably had oceans, but solar radiation gradually boiled the hydrogen and oxygen into space, leaving vast amounts of carbon dioxide. Fuelled by global volcanic activity, Venus has a runaway 'greenhouse effect' that sends surface temperatures soaring to 460 °C (880 °F). Its surface pressure is 92 times Earth's, which is equivalent to being 910 metres (3,000 feet) under our ocean.

*A composite radar map by Magellan shows Venus' 'young' surface – less than 500 million years old and 90% volcanic rock.*

*The only probes to picture the surface of Venus successfully were Russia's tough* Venera *landers.* Venera 13 *(inset) sent this eerie panoramic view of its surroundings.*

## 'HELLISH' SURFACE

Venus is a supremely hostile environment for probes. *Venera 13's* camera windows were made of thick quartz, its instruments encased in a pressure hull and the whole lander was designed to last only 30 minutes while it sent data to its orbiting partner craft. As well as imaging, *Venera 13* analysed a sample of Venusian dirt before imploding in a fiery heap 127 minutes after touchdown. Venus rotates the opposite way to the other planets. It also appears to have a single tectonic plate in its crust, as opposed to Earth's many plates. To solve such mysteries, more probes will go to this shrouded world.

*Venus is pockmarked by 1,600 volcanoes. The 'tick' type, named because it resembles a bug, is unique to the planet.*

**VENUS** spins **more SLOWLY** than any other **planet**. Each **VENUSIAN DAY** lasts **243 Earth** days.

*An artist's impression shows what it might be like to stand on the surface of Venus. As hurricane-force winds scour the surface, lightning arcs down from sulphuric acid clouds, whose droplets vaporise the instant they fall.*

*NASA plans an aerial Venus probe with metal bellows to resist the crushing pressure. It will look for evidence to show how and when Venus' climate became overwhelmed by carbon dioxide.*

# MARS – VIKING

**F**ourth and last of the inner, rocky planets, Mars was the second alien world probed by landers. A global desert, Mars is a half-sized, freeze-dried version of Earth.

*In 1971* Mariner 9 *was the first space probe to orbit Mars. For months a planet-wide dust storm blocked the view. When it cleared* Mariner 9 *was able to map almost the entire planet.*

## INSIDE MARS

1. **ATMOSPHERE** 96% carbon dioxide, 1.9% nitrogen, argon
2. **CRUST** Average 50 km (30 miles) thick
3. **MANTLE** Silicate mineral rocks, similar to Earth's
4. **CORE** Iron and other sulphides, relatively inactive, generates only a weak magnetic field

*Mariner 9 found Mons Olympus, the tallest peak in the Solar System. At 25 km (15 miles) it is three times higher than Everest.*

Our **GRAND CANYON** could **fit** into a **SIDE BRANCH** of **Mars'** great **VALLE MARINARIS.**

*Composite view of Mars, including Valle Marinaris, imaged by the* Viking *orbiter.*

## SCULPTED WORLD

The 1971–72 success of *Mariner 9* spurred NASA to build two combined orbiter/landers for Mars. *Viking 1* reached Mars orbit in June 1976, with *Viking 2* two months later.

*A mock-up* Viking *lander with famous US space expert and cosmologist Carl Sagan.*

The orbiters scanned Mars for landing sites and prepared to act as data relays for their landers. Their searches revealed a world with geological features similar to Earth's – some that could only be explained by torrents of flowing water. Excitement ran high as the two landers were released and de-orbited to begin their descent.

*Mars' atmosphere is so thin, equivalent to 35 km (22 miles) altitude on Earth, that it offers little resistance to landers slowing for touchdown.*

Mariner-based Viking orbiter

**'...we had the audacity to try to soft land on the surface.'** Gentry Lee, chief engineer, NASA/JPL

Viking lander enclosed in heat shield

Viking *landers were sterilised to prevent Mars being contaminated with Earth germs. They used a complex sequence of heat shields, parachutes and landing rockets to arrive safely on the surface.*

**PHOENIX** **OPPORTUNITY** **VIKING 2**

**PATHFINDER** **CURIOSITY**

**VIKING 1** **SPIRIT**

**The** Viking *landers continued to send data for six years. Their success paved the way for many future Martian landers and exploration rovers, as shown above.*

## LIFE ON MARS?

The *Viking* landings were NASA's biggest triumph since the *Apollo* moonshots. As well as imaging, the landers profiled the atmosphere and surface, taking soil samples for analysis in their high-tech, biological mini-laboratories. Some experts believe the results showed evidence of life, but this remains controversial. Because *Viking* was so colossally expensive, following missions had different priorities.

Viking 1 *scooped soil samples from its site in Chryse Planitia, an ancient crater in the Martian lowlands.*

Viking 2 *landed in Utopia Planitia, an area strewn with similar-sized rocks and thought once to be a seabed.*

**VIKING** cost **US $1 BILLION** in **1976** dollars – **US $4 BILLION today**, almost **DOUBLE** the **cost** of **MARS SCIENCE LAB.**

# MARS–MERs

In 1997, NASA sent the first of three robotic Mars Exploration Rovers (MERs) to the Red Planet, starting an exciting new era in Solar System exploration.

*Mars Pathfinder's lander (later renamed Sagan) touched down in 1997. It carried a miniature rover, Sojourner.*

Mars **ORBIT** is **OFF-CENTRE** **compared** with **EARTH** orbit. Each **MARTIAN** **year** lasts **TWO** Earth **YEARS**.

*NASA's Mars missions pioneered a new airbag-cushioned landing method.*

## MOBILE GEOLOGISTS

The success of technologies in 1997's *Mars Pathfinder* led to two bigger MERs, Mars Exploration Rovers, *Spirit* and *Opportunity*. They arrived on the Red Planet in 2004. Their main mission was to search the Martian terrain for evidence of past water activity, and so discover whether the Mars environment was ever favourable to life. The MERs' mission time was set at 90 days and they were not expected to travel more than 600 metres (2,000 feet) from their landing sites.

## MER SYSTEMS

1. **PANORAMIC CAMERAS**
2. **NAVIGATION CAMERAS**
3. **SOLAR ARRAYS**
4. **ROBOT ARM**
5. **MOBILITY SYSTEM** Six one-wheel rocker/bogies, wheels treaded with cleats for grip
6. **BODY** Protects rover battery and electronics, heated by miniature radioisotope generator
7. **ANTENNA** Directional
8. **ANTENNA** Wide beam

*MER's average speed is 10 mm (0.4 inches) per second, halting every 10 seconds to spend 20 seconds analysing the terrain.*

Microscope camera

*Robot arm features an abrasion tool – the rover's version of a geologist's rock hammer and drill.*

Rock abrasion tool

Spectrometer

*Each wheel has its own motor, with the front and rear pairs steerable. The suspension system allows each wheel to climb over rocks twice its height yet keep all six wheels on the ground.*

Far above the rovers, up to four orbiters have been imaging and analysing Mars in ever greater detail. These amazing swirls are Martian dry-ice caps at the North Pole.

**'Their discoveries have revolutionised our view of the Red Planet.'** MER Driver Ashley Stroupe

MARS GLOBAL SURVEYOR

Mars Relay

MARS RECONNAISSANCE ORBITER

Orbiter camera

NASA's Mars Global Surveyor *began orbiting in 1997. It surveyed the surface and acted as a rover relay station until Mars Reconnaissance Orbiter took over in 2006.*

## BEYOND EXPECTATION

Despite the wide-ranging Martian temperatures, from daytime highs of 35 °C (95 °F) to night lows of –143 °C (–225 °F), the MERs performed beautifully. During more than five mission extensions *Spirit* discovered evidence of ancient hot springs, while *Opportunity* fought to free itself from a 'Purgatory' sand dune. Crucially the rovers found twisted rocks and smooth pebbles eroded by water, showing Mars was once even wetter than scientists predicted. After six years and 7.7 km (4.8 miles) of travel, *Spirit* became hopelessly mired in soft sand and ended its mission. *Opportunity* was still roving over 10 years after its arrival.

The MER's heat shield cases opened out flat like petals to allow them to exit in any direction.

In 2010 Opportunity *pictured this Martian 'dust devil' mini-tornado.*

Spirit *photographed its own dust-covered solar panels. Periodic 'cleaning events' – weather – scoured the panels bright again.*

Opportunity *has captured hundreds of detailed Martian panoramic landscapes, like this ancient crater eroded by wind.*

# MARS–CURIOSITY

The latest robot to explore Mars is *Curiosity*, the rover of NASA's *Mars Science Lab*. Its mission is to discover whether Mars has, or has ever had, the means to sustain any form of life.

(1)
(2)

Ultra high frequency antenna

(3)

(7)

High gain antenna

Weather sensor

(4)

*Curiosity's massive tool arm undergoes a systems test at NASA. The rover weighs one tonne (2,204 lb).*

(6)

*Curiosity took this self-portrait at Gale Crater using the Mars Hand Lens Imager on its tool arm, which has a length of two metres (seven feet).*

(5)

Arm joint

## CURIOSITY SYSTEMS

1. **CHEMCAM** Shoots a laser to analyse rock debris
2. **NAVCAMS** Black and white, two each side
3. **TWIN MASTCAMS** High and medium resolution colour, still, video, different filters
4. **SAM** Rock analysis, looking for carbon and other elements essential for life (as we know it)
5. **CHEMIN** Measures levels of all Mars elements
6. **DAN** Radiation detector for subsurface water and ice
7. **BATTERY** Lithium, powered by Multi-Mission Radioisotope Thermoelectric Generator (MMRTG)
8. **MOBILITY** Six one-wheel rocker-bogies, independent drive and suspension, wheels studded with chevron cleats for grip

## SPECIAL DELIVERY

On August 5, 2012 the *Mars Science Lab* capsule sped like a flaming bullet into the Martian atmosphere carrying NASA's latest planet probe. Delivering *Curiosity*, which was the weight of a small 4x4 car, would be a $2.5 billion gamble. Fortunately all went well and the most fully equipped and mobile rover yet – with a top speed of 90 metres (295 feet) per hour! – began its mission.

(8)

*Curiosity's landing site was in the fold of Gale Crater, 160 km (100 miles) wide and formed over 3.5 billion years ago. The crater is rich in minerals and ancient channels, indicating there was once flowing water.*

## 'This mission is a critical planetary science mission...'

NASA Administrator Charles Bolden

*After descending by parachute, the capsule heat shield popped off and a rocket-powered 'skycrane' lowered the Curiosity rover down gently on a nylon cord cradle. After several failed Mars missions, the successful soft landing was a major triumph for NASA.*

# LAB GOES MOBILE

*Curiosity* is a mobile geology and chemistry lab whose primary mission is to look for carbon – the main chemical element that forms the microscopic building-blocks of life. The rover collected, ground up and analysed about 70 samples of soil and rock around Gale Crater. Other work included studying the Martian atmosphere and radiation levels, in case of future human exploration.

The rover travels 4.8–19.3 km (3–12 miles) per day. Based on its early performance, and those of previous rovers, in 2013 *Curiosity*'s mission was extended for several more years – at least.

*The rotating tool head on Curiosity's arm is like a geologist's field kit for rapid, on-the-spot rock analysis.*

Drill

*A tell-tale line of dots shows where CHEMCAM's laser fired into the dust next to a drilling site.*

Alpha Particle X-Ray Spectrometer (APXS)

Mars Hand Lens Imager (MAHLI)

Dust Removal Tool

*Future Mars missions might include bringing samples back to Earth, imagined here with a probe based on the 2005 Phoenix lander.*

**If its nuclear GENERATOR holds out, CURIOSITY could ROAM around MARS for 14 YEARS.**

# JUPITER

Relative size of Earth to Jupiter

**J**upiter and its many moons resemble a solar system in miniature. Shrouded in powerful radiation fields, this giant is effectively a 'nearly' star that wasn't big enough to ignite.

*Veteran space probe Pioneer 10 was the first to visit Jupiter in 1973, learning about the powerful magnetosphere and strange liquid atmosphere of the so-called gas giant.*

## INSIDE JUPITER

1. **AMMONIA CLOUDS**
2. **FLUID HYDROGEN AND HELIUM**
3. **FLUID METALLIC HYDROGEN AND HELIUM** Similar in consistency to the liquid metal mercury
4. **PLANET CORE** Possibly made of iron or rock, or even liquid

## BY JOVE

Jupiter is the next planet after Mars, beyond the Asteroid Belt and at its closest 628 million km (390 million miles) from Earth. NASA's *Pioneer 10* and *11* probes were the first to fly by and photograph, in 1973–74. Then in 1979 Jupiter was visited by NASA's *Voyager 1* and *2* as they headed for the outer Solar System. These missions discovered extra moons, the faint Jovian ring system and filmed the planet's distinctively banded, swirling cloud movements.

**JUPITER** spins so **FAST, 45,300 km/h** (28,300 mph), **that** it has a **huge BULGE** in the **MIDDLE.**

## BENEATH THE SURFACE

In 1989 NASA's *Galileo* probe launched from a US Space Shuttle. Its mission was to orbit the Jupiter system, send an entry probe down into the planet's atmosphere and survey the largest Jovian moons. The results showed that Jupiter contained helium in similar proportions to the Sun and had intense radiation particles above its visible clouds. *Galileo* also sent pictures of Comet Shoemaker-Levy 9 being swallowed up by the gas giant.

*Its main antenna furled shut, Galileo waits to be fitted with upper stage booster rockets at Kennedy Space Center, 1989.*

*This image, clearly showing Jupiter's Great Red Spot, was taken by the Hubble Space Telescope. Earth would fit comfortably inside the huge spot – a storm that is known to have raged for over 300 years.*

**MASSIVE JUPITER** acts like an enormous **space vacuum cleaner**, clearing the **SOLAR SYSTEM** of **dangerous objects**.

*In 2007 NASA's New Horizons probe passed Jupiter on its way to Pluto, capturing images and taking measurements.*

*Galileo's entry probe descended for 59 minutes to a depth of 200 km (125 miles) before disintegrating.*

Main antenna

*Galileo's main antenna refused to deploy (above). So scientists reprogrammed the computers to use the small emergency antenna disk.*

## FIELD STUDIES

In 2000 the *Cassini* probe helped to map and visualise Jupiter's magnetic field and witnessed lightning at the poles, where there are continuous shimmering lights, called auroras. Jupiter also has the most water in the Solar System, which contains particles from when the planet formed. In 2016 NASA's *Juno* probe should orbit close to the surface to analyse these substances. But the radiation field is so strong *Juno* will only last a year before breaking up.

*Juno (right) was launched in 2011. In 2016 it will overfly the polar region to uncover the mystery of the planet's magnetic 'dynamo'.*

# SATURN

**P**ale yellow Saturn is the furthest planet visible with the naked eye. This gas giant is celebrated for its amazing ring system, whose secrets are being revealed by the *Cassini/Huygens* mission.

① ② ③ ④

## INSIDE SATURN

1. **UPPER ATMOSPHERE** Traces of ammonia and methane
2. **MAIN ATMOSPHERE** Hydrogen 97%, helium 3%
3. **CORE** Probably a thick metallic form of hydrogen, possibly with a small rocky core about the size of Earth at its centre
4. **PLANETARY RING SYSTEM** with Cassini Gap

Some **SCIENTISTS** think **SATURN** provides a **MODEL** of **how** our **SOLAR SYSTEM** formed about **4.6 BILLION YEARS ago**.

*Saturn's polar region has an unusual six-sided cloud system. The eye of the red-coloured vortex is 20 times larger than Earth's biggest hurricane.*

*The* Cassini *probe is named after 17th-century astronomer Giovanni Cassini. In 2004 it went into Saturn orbit and released the* Huygens *lander to touch down on Titan.* Cassini *will end its mission with a controlled fall into Saturn's atmosphere in 2017.*

## MASSIVELY LIGHT

Although smaller than Jupiter, Saturn is still gigantic – 760 Earths could fit inside. Internally it is similar to Jupiter, but with a cooler, less angry climate. Ammonia crystals in the upper atmosphere colour the planet pale yellow. Its average temperature is –178 ˚C (–288 ˚F). Saturn's awesome rings are made up of billions of pure ice fragments, probably the remnants of destroyed moons. More than 50 Saturnian moons have been named.

Magnetometer boom

Radio/plasma wave subsystem antennae

Radioisotope thermoelectric generator (RTG)

Rocket engines

*Huygens* probe

Cooling fins

Antenna system

*Like other deep space craft,* Cassini *uses heat from radioactive decay to generate electricity.*

> **'Cassini *has shown us how active and ever-changing Saturn is.*'** Linda Spilker, Cassini project scientist at JPL

## GIRDLED BY MOONS

*The moon Enceladus may contain salt oceans under its surface.*

Titan, the largest of Saturn's moons, is big enough to hold an atmosphere. In 2005 *Huygens* successfully landed there (see page 24). The other moons vary greatly. Many, like Dione, are a mixture of rock and hard ice. Iapetus is clean on one side and spattered with soot from impacts on the other. Hyperion is shaped like a potato – possibly a comet captured by Saturn's gravity.

Some of the moons play a key role in shaping Saturn's fabulous rings. The orbit of Mimas pulls particles towards it, creating a gap called the Cassini Division. Other moons, like Prometheus and Pandora, orbit inside the rings and keep them in shape. *Cassini* is now on an extended mission, studying the intricate Saturnian system.

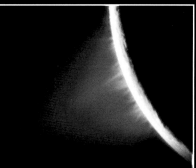

*Cassini made a great discovery by imaging Enceladus venting geysers of water ice into space. The ring it inhabits has been made by the moon itself.*

*Viewed by* **Cassini**, *Mimas is shown against the majesty of Saturn's rings. This moon orbits well outside the rings. It has a huge crater from an ancient impact that nearly split it in half.*

**Cassini***'s Saturn orbits have analysed the density of ring particles. The icy pieces constantly collide with each other, shattering to make new surfaces that keep the rings shining brightly.*

Puck

*Due to an ancient collision with an Earth-sized planet, Uranus rotates with its axis at an angle of 82°. Circled by rings and moons, it resembles a celestial ferris wheel when viewed by the Hubble Space Telescope.*

Juliet

Miranda

Ariel

**O**ften called 'ice giants', the two outermost planets are mysterious, frozen worlds. One is tipped crazily on its side, the other has ferocious, roaring winds.

*Uranus' moon Miranda is a bizarre world of shattered and reformed ice canyons and ridges. One of these, Verona Rupes (indicated), is twice as high as Earth's Mount Everest.*

## INSIDE URANUS AND NEPTUNE

1. **OUTER LAYERS** Hydrogen, helium, methane, with a thick hydrocarbon haze obscuring Uranus' clouds
2. **MANTLE** Water, ammonia and methane ices
3. **CORE** Rock and ice

1

2

3

Size of Earth

Scientific instruments

Antenna

*The two Voyager spacecraft are both the size of a small house. They were launched to take advantage of a rare alignment of the planets that happens once every 177 years. Each craft is powered by three radioisotope thermoelectric generators (RTGs).*

Message from Earth

RTGs

The **RINGS** of **URANUS** are the **DARKEST** objects in the **SOLAR SYSTEM**.

## TO THE ICE GIANTS

Uranus and Neptune are similar in size, and also similar internally to the other gas giants, except their mantles are made of chemical ices rather than metallic hydrogen. The only probe to visit was *Voyager 2*, which left Earth in 1977, reaching Uranus in 1986. *Voyager* pictured the planet as a featureless pale greenish-blue globe. Coldest planet in the Solar System, Uranus can drop to −192 °C (−323 °F), but why it gives out so little heat is a mystery. Uranus also has 27 moons – cracked, cratered miniworlds of rock and ice.

*Uranus finally revealed some surface features in 2005 when the Sun passed over its equator and also highlighted its ring edges. One Uranus orbit lasts 84.3 Earth years.*

The largest of Neptune's 14 moons and the only one that is a sphere, Triton was visited close-up by Voyager 2. Thought to be a captured Kuiper Belt object (see page 28) it spins the opposite way to nearly every other planetary moon. Triton is slowly falling in orbit towards Neptune and ultimate destruction – in 3 billion years' time. The coldest body in the Solar System, it shoots out liquid nitrogen in geyser-like fountains.

# STORM GIANT

Before it was seen, Neptune, the eighth and outermost planet, was discerned by calculations based on the orbital path of Uranus. *Voyager 2* arrived in 1989 to find a blue world (due to methane) with banded clouds and storm spots that race over the surface. Neptune has the highest sustained winds of any planet – up to 1,448 km/h (900 mph). It has similar spin tilt to Earth, 28.3° but its orbit takes 165 of our years and it receives only 1/1,000th of the sunlight here on Earth. With such wild weather, its rain might be in the form of methane crystal 'diamonds'.

*A great dark spot, roughly the size of Earth, was seen by* Voyager *on Neptune. Neptune's spots are churning pressure storms that tear deep holes in the outer atmosphere, revealing the mantle below.*

*Neptune's faint and fragmentary ring system was imaged by* Voyager 2.

**VOYAGER 2** is now **leaving** the **SOLAR SYSTEM** to **probe INTERSTELLAR SPACE** until **2025,** when its **power** will **DIE**.

# PLANETARY MOONS

**F**rom bundles of space rubble to mysterious ice worlds that may harbour life, space exploration has revealed amazing variety in the 170-plus known planetary satellites of the Solar System.

*Phobos, the largest of Mars' twin moons, orbits its parent planet closer than any other moon. In less than 50 million years time it will break up in the Martian atmosphere and become a planetary ring. Mars Reconnaissance Orbiter took close-up views of Phobos in 2007–08, revealing its dusty surface.*

RADAR

High gain antenna

PHOBOS

Spectrometer

Imaging camera

## A FROZEN EARTH?

Mars' twin moons, Phobos and Deimos, may well be captured asteroids. Other moons are created when material hurtling in the orbit of a newborn planet clumps together and builds up until there is enough mass for the moon to become a sphere. This is probably what happened with Saturn's moon Titan – the only moon in the Solar System to have a thick atmosphere. In 2005 the *Huygens* probe landed on Titan as part of the *Cassini* mission (see page 20). As *Huygens* floated down on a parachute through the atmosphere, it saw a world that was alien, yet eerily familiar.

*Huygens operated in temperatures of –180 °C (–356 °F).*

*Titan is the second largest moon in the Solar System.*

*Titan's upper atmosphere is 98.4% nitrogen, visible as a thin blue line (left). The only other nitrogen-rich atmosphere is Earth's. The moon's landscape is also strangely Earth-like (right). Scientists believe Titan resembles a primordial version of Earth, but deep-frozen, with a methane cycle instead of a water cycle.*

*Titan's liquid methane raindrops fall like snowflakes in its low gravity and collect in lakes.*

① 

## INSIDE EUROPA?

1. **ICE SURFACE** Cold -145 °C (-200 °F) and brittle, seen to rotate independently of planet interior
2. **SUBSURFACE WATER** Liquid or slush convecting ice
3. **MANTLE** Rocky minerals
4. **CORE** Metallic elements

## WATERWORLD?

*Could Europa's distinctive stained cracks be caused by types of primitive bacteria?*

Jupiter's four largest, or Galilean, moons were first observed by astronomer Galileo in 1610. The second of these, icy Europa, has become a focus in the search for extraterrestrial life. Europa follows an elliptical (egg-shaped) orbit around Jupiter, causing tidal forces to stretch the moon. This heats and possibly melts its interior ice to make a subsurface salt-water ocean. Life flourishes on Earth in extreme cold with no sunlight – why not Europa? Europa could contain more water than all of Earth's oceans put together, *if* the clues on its surface hold true.

Galilean moons

Io    Europa    Ganymede    Callisto

*Io is a volcanic world tortured inside by its closeness to Jupiter's gravitational pull. Ganymede is the largest moon in the Solar System – bigger than planet Mercury. Of the four, only Callisto remains untouched by Jupiter's intense radiation.*

*Europa's frozen surface (above) shows a cracked landscape similar to ice floes on Earth. The artist's impression below shows Jupiter as seen from the surface of Europa. ESA is planning to send a probe to Jupiter's icy moons in 2022.*

**EUROPA's ICE SURFACE makes it the SMOOTHEST object in the SOLAR SYSTEM.**

# ASTEROIDS AND COMETS

**A**steroids are space rocks – leftovers from the Solar System's formation. Comets are icy bodies that are pulled in by the Sun's gravity from a distant realm way beyond Neptune.

*The first asteroid orbited by spacecraft was 433 Eros, visited by* **NEAR** *(Near Earth Asteroid Rendezvous)* **Shoemaker** *in 2000. Eros was found to be a solid object about 4.5 billion years old.*

Solar arrays

Asteroid Eros

Magnetometer

Scientific instruments around base

## ROCK HUNTERS

Eros is about the size of the asteroid thought to have wiped out the dinosaurs on Earth 66 million years ago. Over 10,000 NEAs, Near Earth Asteroids, discovered so far have come from the Asteroid Belt, a thinly dispersed zone of debris between Mars and Jupiter. Asteroids range in size from dusty specks to the four largest – Hygiea, Pallas, Vesta and dwarf planet Ceres. Together these form about half the mass of the Asteroid Belt. Scientists classify asteroids as carbon (C-type), silicate (S-type), or metal rich (M-type), depending on their content.

*NEAR Shoemaker made a successful touchdown on Eros and found a thick layer of regolith – dirt and debris, similar to moondust.*

*The Asteroid Belt probe* **Dawn** *visited Vesta (above) in 2011 and found a rocky body similar to a terrestrial world.* **Dawn** *will go on to orbit Ceres in 2015, which resembles an ice world. This should show why asteroids evolved so differently.*

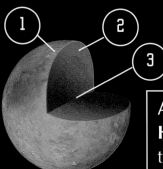

**ASTEROIDS** give us **clues** about **HOW** planets **FORMED** and **why** they **EVOLVED** in **certain ways**.

## INSIDE CERES

1. **CRUST** Thin, dusty
2. **MANTLE** Water ice
3. **CORE** Rocky minerals

*In 2010 Japan's* **Hayabusa** *probe returned samples from asteroid 25143 Itokawa to Earth. A more ambitious concept is to capture a whole Near Earth Asteroid and place it in orbit around the Moon. The NEA could then be mined for its valuable mineral content.*

## 'Prior to Deep Impact *we had almost no real knowledge of a comet's nucleus.'* Principal Investigator Prof Michael A'Hearn

*As comets near the Sun, the solar wind vaporises their solids to make a glow or coma around the head, and a long, fiery tail. Comets were long seen as signs of doom. In 1066 Halley's Comet appeared before England's fateful Battle of Hastings.*

GIOTTO

*Halley passes Earth every 75 years and was studied up close by probe* Giotto *in 1986.* Giotto *found dusty black rock with less ice than expected.*

DEEP IMPACT

*In 2005 NASA's flyby probe* **Deep Impact** *released a small impacter to hit the surface of comet Tempel 3 (above). The cloud of ejected material was then analysed revealing a surface like 'talcum powder'.*

Sample return capsule

High resolution imager

Impacter

STARDUST

*In 1999 NASA's Stardust probe flew into the coma of Comet Wild 2 and collected a sample of dust which was automatically returned to Earth in a capsule.*

A long-standing **THEORY says** that an **ancient COMET IMPACT** may have brought **LIFE** to **EARTH.**

## COMET CHASERS

Comets are 'icy rockballs', studied for their volatile (low boiling point) materials encased in loose build-ups of rock. They vary in size from 0.8 km (0.5 miles) to dozens of times larger. Their journeys around the Sun also vary greatly, from less than 200 years (short period comets) to millennia (long period comets). Most known comets came from the Kuiper Belt beyond Neptune (see page 29). Long period comets travel from the very edge of the Solar System, to be seen only once in recorded history. These mini-worlds offer a direct look at the Solar System's origins.

*In 2014 ESA's orbiter* Rosetta *will release a lander onto comet 67P/Churyumov-Gerasimenko to gather samples as it breaks up on its approach to the Sun.*

27

# BEYOND THE PLANETS

**I**n 2006 Pluto was demoted to dwarf planet status – a new category of world, massive enough to become spherical but lacking the gravity to make a clear orbital path.

## NEW HORIZONS SYSTEMS

1. **RTG** Radioisotope Thermoelectric Generator
2. **REX** Radiometer measures atmosphere
3. **PEPSSI** Analyses atmospheric ions (particles)
4. **SWAP** Solar wind and plasma recorder
5. **LORRI** Telescopic reconnaissance camera
6. **SDC** Counts amount of space dust on the probe

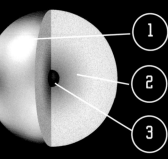

## INSIDE PLUTO

1. **SURFACE** Nitrogen, methane ice and frosts with seasonal melting
2. **MANTLE** Mixed rocks and ice
3. **CORE** Small, probably rocky

*Pluto seen from the Hubble Space Telescope is a vague mass of light and dark.*

## DWARF WORLD

NASA's deep space probe *New Horizons* left Earth in 2004 to arrive at Pluto in 2015, with a closest approach of 12,500 km (7,800 miles). Scientists expect to see a rocky ice world with landscape features and a hazy nitrogen-based atmosphere. Pluto's orbit passes through the Kuiper Belt, a debris field of leftover material from the formation of the Solar System, where more dwarf planets have been discovered. Pluto has five known moons, the last discovered in 2012. It spins on its side, like Uranus, and rotates backwards, like Venus, and does both slowly – one Plutonian day lasts 6.5 Earth days and one year is 247.7 Earth years.

CHARON

High gain antenna (hidden)

1
2
3
4

Radiation shield

5

Ultraviolet imaging spectrometer (hidden)

6

Visible/infrared imager/spectrometer

PLUTO is **15 times** more **MASSIVE** than **CERES**, our **nearest** dwarf **PLANET**.

*Pluto's largest moon, Charon, is one-eighth of its mass; Earth's Moon is one-eightieth of Earth's mass. Charon also orbits 20 times closer than our Moon orbits us. This makes Pluto and Charon tidally locked, spinning around as if tied by rope, always showing each other the same faces.*

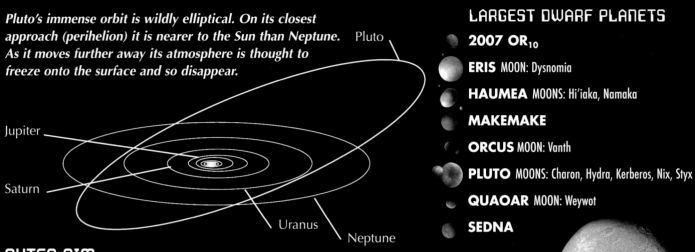

*Pluto's immense orbit is wildly elliptical. On its closest approach (perihelion) it is nearer to the Sun than Neptune. As it moves further away its atmosphere is thought to freeze onto the surface and so disappear.*

Pluto

Jupiter

Saturn

Uranus

Neptune

## LARGEST DWARF PLANETS

**2007 OR$_{10}$**

**ERIS** MOON: Dysnomia

**HAUMEA** MOONS: Hi'iaka, Namaka

**MAKEMAKE**

**ORCUS** MOON: Vanth

**PLUTO** MOONS: Charon, Hydra, Kerberos, Nix, Styx

**QUAOAR** MOON: Weywot

**SEDNA**

*Eris is currently the largest dwarf planet. Its orbit takes 557 Earth years.*

# OUTER RIM

After flying by Pluto, *New Horizons* will travel onwards to the doughnut-shaped Kuiper Belt. This outer realm may contain thousands more dwarf planets. Several have been discovered in recent years, although only the largest are named so far. Distant Sedna's orbit of over 11,000 Earth years takes it close to the farthest, coldest zone of the Solar System, the Oort Cloud. This has never been seen.

But scientists use evidence from long period comets to theorise that the Oort Cloud may be like a much larger Kuiper Belt, but expanded as a vast spherical shell – truly the final frontier.

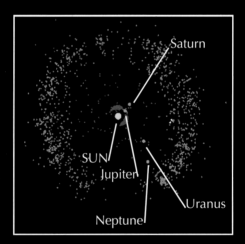

Saturn

SUN

Jupiter

Uranus

Neptune

*The Kuiper Belt is shaped like a doughnut or flattened disc. Comets from this region travel around the Sun on the same plane as the planets.*

**BEYOND** the **KUIPER BELT** there **could** be as **many** as a **TRILLION** dwarf **planets** in the **OORT CLOUD.**

*This artist's impression shows summer on Pluto. The surface frosts have evaporated and risen to form a haze. Pluto's weak gravity (one-sixth of Earth's) allows this thin atmosphere to spread far out into space.*

# TECH FILES – SOLAR SYSTEM

## SUN

**DIAMETER** 1.39 million km (865,000 miles)
**MASS** 333,000 times more massive than Earth
**SURFACE TEMPERATURE** 5,500 °C (9,930 °F)
**ATMOSPHERE** 73.5% hydrogen, 24.8% helium, oxygen and other trace elements

## MERCURY

**DIAMETER** 4,879 km (3,032 miles)
**MASS** 5.5% of Earth mass
**TEMPERATURE** 427 °C (800 °F) to -173 °C (-280 °F)
**ATMOSPHERE** Trace amounts of hydrogen and helium
**LENGTH OF DAY** 58.6 Earth days
**LENGTH OF YEAR** 87.9 Earth years
**DISTANCE FROM THE SUN** Min 48.9 million km (28.5 million miles), max 69.8 million km (43.5 million miles)

## VENUS

**DIAMETER** 12,100 km (7,518 miles)
**MASS** 81% of Earth mass
**TEMPERATURE** Near constant 460 °C (860 °F)
**ATMOSPHERE** 96% carbon dioxide, 3% nitrogen, 0.1% water vapour
**LENGTH OF DAY** 243 Earth days
**LENGTH OF YEAR** 224.7 Earth days
**DISTANCE FROM THE SUN** Average 108 million km (67 million miles)

## EARTH

**DIAMETER** 12,756 km (7,926 miles)
**MASS** Almost 6,000 billion billion tons
**TEMPERATURE** Average range 37 °C (98 °F) to -13 °C (-8 °F)
**ATMOSPHERE** 78% nitrogen, 21% oxygen, 1% argon
**LENGTH OF DAY** 23.93 hours
**LENGTH OF YEAR** 365 days
**MOONS:** 1
**DISTANCE FROM THE SUN** Average 149.5 million km (92.9 million miles)

## MARS

**DIAMETER** 6,787 km (4,217 miles)
**MASS** 10% of Earth's mass
**TEMPERATURE** 37 °C (98 °F) to -123 °C (-190 °F)
**ATMOSPHERE** 96% carbon dioxide, 1.9% nitrogen, 1.9% argon
**LENGTH OF DAY** 24.4 Earth hours
**LENGTH OF YEAR** 686.9 Earth days
**MOONS:** 2
**DISTANCE FROM THE SUN** Average 227.9 million km (141.6 million miles)

## JUPITER

**DIAMETER** 142,800 km (88,731 miles)
**MASS** 317 times more massive than Earth
**TEMPERATURE** Average at the cloud tops -153 °C (-243 °F)
**ATMOSPHERE** 90% hydrogen, 10% helium, 0.07% methane
**LENGTH OF DAY** 9.8 Earth hours
**LENGTH OF YEAR** 11.7 Earth years
**MOONS:** 65-plus, also faint rings
**DISTANCE FROM THE SUN** 778.4 million km (483.6 million miles)

## SATURN

**DIAMETER** 120,660 km (74,974 miles)
**MASS** 95 times more massive than Earth
**TEMPERATURE** -185 °C (-301 °F) at equivalent of Earth's sea level pressure
**ATMOSPHERE** 97% hydrogen, 3% helium, 0.05% methane
**LENGTH OF DAY** 10.2 Earth hours
**LENGTH OF YEAR** 29.5 Earth years
**MOONS:** Over 60, also extensive ring system
**DISTANCE FROM THE SUN** 1,426.7 million km (886.5 million miles)

## URANUS

**DIAMETER** 51,118 km (31,763 miles)
**MASS** 14.5 times more massive than Earth
**TEMPERATURE** -192 °C (-323 °F)
**ATMOSPHERE** 83% hydrogen, 15% helium, 2% methane (at depth)
**LENGTH OF DAY** 17.9 Earth hours
**LENGTH OF YEAR** 84.3 Earth years
**MOONS:** 27, also dark ring system
**DISTANCE FROM THE SUN** 2.8 billion km (1.7 billion miles)

## NEPTUNE

**DIAMETER** 49,528 km (30,775 miles)
**MASS** 17 times more massive than Earth
**TEMPERATURE** -225 °C (-373 °F)
**ATMOSPHERE** 74% hydrogen, 25% helium, 1% methane (at depth)
**LENGTH OF DAY** 19.1 Earth hours
**LENGTH OF YEAR** 164.8 Earth years
**MOONS:** 14 , also faint rings
**DISTANCE FROM THE SUN** 4.4 billion km (2.8 billion miles)

*Planets and Sun accurate for diameter scale but not distance

THE SUN

Mercury  Venus  Earth  Mars

Jupiter      Saturn

Uranus      Neptune

# GLOSSARY

**ASTEROID** relatively small, rocky or metallic space object orbiting the Sun; most are between 10 m (33 feet) and 1,000 km (620 miles) across

**ATMOSPHERE** layer of gases around a space object such as a planet

**COMET** relatively small space object following a long, lop-sided orbit around the Sun, that warms and glows when near the Sun

**CORE** dense central region of a star, planet, moon or similar space object

**CORONA** intensely hot region, usually of plasma, around space objects such as stars

**CRUST** hard outermost layer of a planet, moon or similar space object

**DWARF PLANET** space object that orbits a star but has not cleared its orbit of other large objects

**ELLIPTICAL** oval-shaped, as for the orbits of many planets

**FUSION** in nuclear fusion, parts of atoms combine or join and give off energy, as when hydrogen atoms fuse into helium in the Sun

**GRAVITY** force of attraction between objects, which is especially huge for massive objects like planets and stars

**MANTLE** middle region, between the crust and core, of a planet, moon or similar space object

**MASS** amount of matter in an object, in the form of numbers and kinds of atoms

**MOON** space object that orbits a planet

**ORBIT** regular path of one object around a larger one, determined by the speed, mass and gravity of the objects

**PLANET** large space object that has a spherical shape due to its gravity, and has cleared a regular orbital path around a star

**PLASMA** One of four basic states of matter, similar to gas but the atoms or other particles have electrical charges, positive or negative

**PLATE TECTONICS** system of large, rigid, curved, interlocking, slow-moving plates that form the surface of Earth and certain other planets

**SATELLITE** space object that goes around or orbits another, including natural satellites like the Moon orbiting Earth or Earth orbiting the Sun, and man-made satellites

**STAR** space object that at some stage is large and dense enough, with enough gravity, to undergo fusion and give out light, heat and similar energy

# INDEX